# my father said

# my father said

RYLAND

PETERS

& SMALL

LONDON NEW YORK

Designers: Sonya Nathoo and Sarah Rock

Senior editor: Catherine Osborne

Picture research: Emily Westlake

Production manager: Patricia Harrington

Art director: Leslie Harrington

Publishing director: Alison Starling

First published in the United States in 2008 by
Ryland Peters & Small, Inc.
519 Broadway, 5th Floor
New York, NY 10012
www.rylandpeters.com

ISBN 978 1 84597 641 5

# contents

# my father said...

If you thought that fathers were the last people to turn to for advice, then think again. It's at times when you perhaps least expect it that your father's words of wisdom ring loud and clear– "Measure twice, cut once," "Plenty more fish in the sea," "Don't ask and you won't get," "Money doesn't grow on trees." From do-it-yourself disasters and dates from hell to career crises and money troubles, fathers have always been there to offer guidance, whether you've asked for it or not. They may be blunt and off-hand, but we all know deep down that our fathers only have our best interests at heart. "What doesn't kill you, only makes you stronger!"

# growing up

*It is a wise father that knows his own child.*

WILLIAM SHAKESPEARE

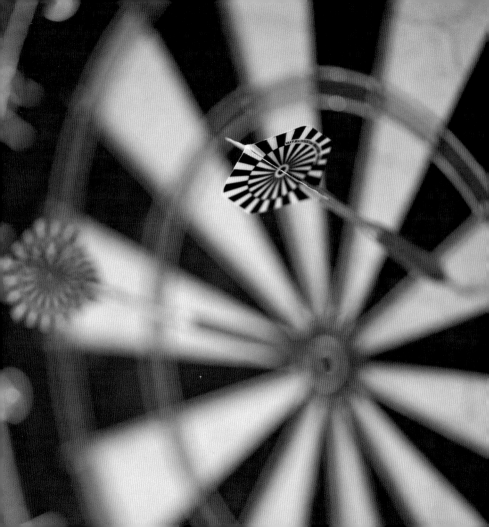

BEING the only girl among five brothers I was teased a lot and frequently lost my cool. My father told me if I just ignored their taunts they would eventually get bored because they weren't getting a reaction. Following this advice made me a stronger person, and I have since applied it to similar situations in my adulthood.

IF you haven't got something good to say about someone, then don't say anything at all.

MEN are like buses. Just wait on the corner and another one will come along.

WHAT doesn't kill you, only makes you stronger.

ENGAGE your brain before opening your mouth.

YOU'RE not leaving the table until you've
finished what's on your plate!

WHEN I was younger, I was always getting into trouble.
My father had the patience of a saint and never raised his
voice to me. Instead he always calmly asked why I'd
committed my latest act of rebellion. When I couldn't come
up with a reasonable answer, I knew I was in the wrong.

TWO wrongs do not make a right.

THROUGHOUT my teenage years, my dad told me never to join the Army (he was in the forces) or get a motorbike. However, some years later he raved about how good the Swiss Army were because they had a mountain motorbike division.

*"Don't ask me. Ask your mother."* The art of avoidance– something my father trained me well in.

IF you think life's hard now, wait until you get to my age!

FATHER to daughter: "If anyone bothers you, kick them where it hurts and run like hell."

DON'T do as I do, do as you're told.

# home improvement

*It is impossible to please all the world and one's father.*

Jean de La Fontaine (1621–1695)

BEFORE I left to go to college, my father bought me a toolbox, which at the time I thought was a bit of an odd gift, especially as I was the kind of daughter who was more likely to use it as a place to store my makeup. I didn't have a clue what half the things in there were, but by the end of my first year away from home I could quite happily tell the difference between a wrench, screwdriver, and a pair of pliers. I still have the toolbox, and I have my father to thank for my ability to put up a flat-packed wardrobe in record time!

MY father always taught me the importance of following instructions. I'm reminded of this every time I attempt to work my camera without reading the manual first and wonder why I get images of people with red eyes.

A LITTLE dirt never hurt anyone.

YOU won't get a good finish unless you start off properly.

NEVER tackle a big job so late that you can't finish it the same day.

IF it ain't broke, don't fix it.

IF you want something done properly do it yourself.

*"IF it doesn't fit, don't force it."* A very sound piece of advice my father gave me after one too many do-it-yourself disasters!

PREPARATION is 90% of the work.

DON'T rush. If you're going to do a job properly, take the time to do it well. There's nothing more unsightly than poor workmanship.

MEASURE twice,
cut once.

# life's ups and downs

*Love and fear. Everything the father of
a family says must inspire one or the other.*

JOSEPH JOUBERT (1754–1824)

PRIDE comes before a fall.

LIFE is all about timing.

IF you run away from your problems, they'll
have a horrible habit of catching up with you.
Face them head on.

WHEN I started my first job after graduating, I had to work with some particularly bullish characters and took a lot of what they said to heart. My father's advice at the time was, *"Never let anyone tell you that you're not good enough."* Whenever I feel myself reaching the end of my tether, I keep these words in mind. It's helped me keep my spirits up even when all around me is chaos, and everyone else is ready to give up.

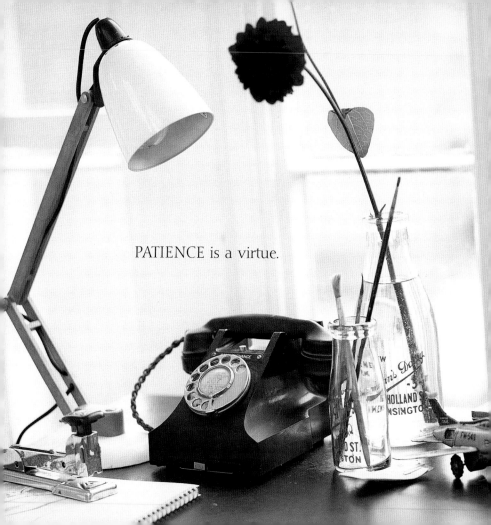

PATIENCE is a virtue.

YOU win some,
you lose some.

FATHER to son: "Never ask a woman for an explanation."

IF I was ever feeling a bit low about something my father always said, *"It's better than a poke in the eye with a blunt stick."*

YOU can't always be right.

BEAUTY is in the eye of the beholder.

WHEN I was younger I was absolutely hopeless at math. My father would sit down with me at the kitchen table and go through problem by problem until I got one right. Whenever he sensed I was about to give up, he would tell me, *"If you think you can't do it, you won't. Calm down and think things through."* Now whenever I'm about to give up on something I remember my math homework. I am, however, still hopeless with numbers!

THREE strikes and you're out!

SOMETIMES winning is taking a step
back and admitting defeat.

DON'T go looking for trouble because
trouble will have no problem finding you.

LIVE life to the full. Just don't wear
yourself out doing it.

# money,
# money, money

*A truly rich man is one whose children run
into his arms when his hands are empty.*

Author Unknown

*"I WANT, doesn't get!"* I remember going through a particularly annoying stage as a child when I expected my parents to buy me everything and anything I wanted. This was always my father's retort. I eventually learned that receiving things unexpectedly was a much more fulfilling experience.

MONEY doesn't grow on trees!

IF you invest in one thing in life,
invest in property.

IF he doesn't offer to pay for dinner,
he's not worth it.

WORK for yourself, and not for
anyone else.

NEVER say *"no"* to a good bargain.

NOTHING in life is free. There's always a catch.

I DIDN'T get where I am today by sitting back and doing nothing. You've got to work hard to get somewhere in life.

*"IF you can't afford it, don't buy it."* Something my father told me as a child and is still telling me to this day. What can I say, that nice leather handbag just had my name on it!

Father to daughter: "Never leave all money matters to the man and remain in ignorance (or you might get a nasty surprise one day)."

# love and laughter

*There are three stages of a man's life: He believes in Santa Claus,
he doesn't believe in Santa Claus, he is Santa Claus.*

AUTHOR UNKNOWN

WHENEVER I went out on a date, my father always told me that I should go out of my way to make her feel comfortable and appreciated, whether that was through opening a car door for her or paying for a meal. Although I thought this was slightly old-fashioned advice at the time, it has certainly helped me have some very successful dates!

LAUGHTER is the best form of therapy.

STICK a plaster on it, and it'll be fine!

ALWAYS wear clean underwear!

MY father once gave me some very blunt but apt advice. *"Not everyone in life is as nice as you are. You may learn this the hard way, but you'll eventually wise up."* Now when I find myself in stressful situations with people, I've learned not to expect an easy or pleasant way out.

DURING my teenage years I went through many boyfriends, who of course all broke my heart. My mother was always there with the tissues, while my father could be heard in the background uttering, *"There's plenty more fish in the sea."* This did little to ease my pain at the time, but now that I'm older I can certainly see the truth in that statement.

A MAN who can cook will always be popular with the ladies.

NEVER mix your drinks, unless you want to end up naked and tied to a lamppost.

FATHER to son: "If you want to know what your girlfriend will be like in years to come, take a long hard look at her mother."

Make sure you see the world before you settle down. Once you have children you're committed to them for the next 18 years, and you can't take them with you.

YOU can't pick your family, but you can pick your friends. Choose wisely.

TREAT them mean, keep them keen.

FRIENDS come and go, and only the best stay by you through thick and thin.

NEVER forget your mom's birthday. She may not say anything, but she certainly won't forget it!

# picture credits

Winfried Heinze 10, 25, 36, 39, 51, 62 (Lisa Jackson Ltd – LCJPeace@aol.com);
Tom Leighton 1 & 57 (www.rogeroates.co.uk), 29, 35; Debi Treloar 17, 18, 44, 61
(www.asfourguzy.com); Chris Everard 6, 32, 54; James Merrell 4-5, 14, 20; Caroline Arber
3 & 8 (www.caroline-zoob.co.uk); Chris Tubbs 40, 52; Polly Wreford 2, 42; Jan Baldwin 48;
Martin Brigdale 58; Peter Cassidy 30; Christopher Drake 26; Dan Duchars 22
(www.smithcreative.net); Alan Williams 47; Andrew Wood 13 (www.kjaerholms.dk).


Thank you to Clare Double, Celine Hughes, Cindy Richards,
Richard Sandom-Brown, Paul Tilby, Emily Westlake, and all the other sons and daughters
who contributed to this book.